SING

But Keep On Walking

Dedicated to Tom, Katy, Linus, Erin and Ailidh,
who play instruments and play with words,
sing joyfully and keep on walking into the future.

SING

But Keep On Walking

Readings, poems and prayers for Advent

Jan Sutch Pickard

wild goose
publications

www.**ionabooks**.com

Copyright © 2019 Jan Sutch Pickard

First published 2019

Wild Goose Publications
21 Carlton Court, Glasgow G5 9JP, UK
www.ionabooks.com
Wild Goose Publications is the publishing division of the Iona Community.
Scottish Charity No. SC003794. Limited Company Reg. No. SC096243.

ISBN 978-1-84952-696-8
Cover image © Swkunst | Dreamstime.com

Overseas distribution:
Australia: Willow Connection Pty Ltd, Unit 4A, 3-9 Kenneth Road,
Manly Vale, NSW 2093
New Zealand: Pleroma, Higginson Street, Otane 4170, Central Hawkes Bay
Canada: Novalis/Bayard Publishing & Distribution, 10 Lower Spadina Ave.,
Suite 400, Toronto, Ontario M5V 2Z2

Printed by Bell & Bain, Thornliebank, Glasgow

CONTENTS

INTRODUCTION

A few years ago I enjoyed writing, for Wild Goose, a book of reflections called *Walking through Advent*. I'm still walking – though more slowly now (I am getting older). And I try to keep on singing, joining my voice with others (as in the psalms published in the *Iona Abbey Worship Book*) and also finding my own words in poems and prayers and storytelling.

This sequence of reflections has all of those. It moves between the islands of Mull and Iona, and the hills of the West Bank and Jerusalem. Some images recur – like flocks of migrating birds or flowing water, like stories of people who work with their hands: sculptors, a carpenter, a baker. There are real people here, whose lives I want to celebrate, though not all of them are named.

I'm writing amid political chaos and climate crisis, with no easy answers. I barely mention the big issues – but they're there. We can't ignore them. But we can speak truth to power, walk side by side, sing justice; we can live an alternative. No man or woman is an island, and *'No one is too small to make a difference'* (Greta Thunberg) in a time like this.

A time for panic and a time for hope,
of urgency with much uncertainty,
of waiting and impatience;
a time of looking forward and a time for looking back,
awareness of our mortality,
with eagerness to celebrate new life.

A time for prophecy
and for practical preparations;

a time for silence and a time for singing,
a time for stillness and a time for travelling on;

when plants die while seeds and corms store spring;
when the safe and familiar give way to wonder.

As migrating flocks cross our skies,
constellations wheel with the turning year;
the story of the seasons,
the story of salvation –
Advent and Christmas, Lent and Easter, Pentecost –
the song never ends.

A time of too many expectations,
and a time of deep expectancy;
a time for being human together,
and a time to celebrate God-with-us:
Incarnation. Amen

Jan Sutch Pickard

SING BUT KEEP ON WALKING

It is good to sing to God,
to offer heartfelt praise.

(From Psalm 147, *Iona Abbey Worship Book*)

As I walked my way to health in Advent 2013, a friend sent me this translation of words from Augustine of Hippo, written as part of a sermon in the third century AD:

So brethren, let us sing Alleluia,
not in the enjoyment of heavenly rest, but to sweeten our toil.
Sing as travellers sing along the road: but keep walking.
Solace your toil by singing – do not yield to idleness.
Sing but keep on walking.

What do I mean by walking?
I mean press on from good to better.
The apostle says there are some who go from bad to worse.
But if you press on, you keep on walking.
Go forward then in virtue, in true faith and right conduct.
Sing up – and keep on walking.
People travel to wonder at the height of the mountains,
at the huge waves of the sea and at the long courses of rivers,
at the vast compass of the ocean, at the circular motion of the stars.
And they pass by themselves without wondering …

I like the way that this extract ends with a glimpse of 3rd-century tourists, keen to see the wonders of the world, but learning nothing about themselves: *'they pass by themselves without wondering'*! God calls us to set out on a journey, but it is an inner and outer journey. This could be a positive experience, where singing on the way is the most natural thing in the world. I imagine the pilgrimages to Jerusalem in which Jesus and his family joined when he was a child: there must have been singing among the crowds on the road, psalms of pilgrimage.

But when Mary made her way to visit her cousin Elizabeth, maybe still in shock or beginning to reflect with wonder on the angel's news, did she sing? Or was this experience beyond words?

When, heavily pregnant, she made her way with Joseph to Bethlehem, not knowing when or where her baby would be born, did they feel like singing – did any of the other displaced people on the road sing? Yet at a time like this – or on a protest march – singing is the thing that can give courage and a sense of community.

> *O God, you challenge us to pilgrimage,*
> *and you walk with us on those journeys we did not choose.*
> *Keep us singing: with joy, with courage, with hope.*
> *Amen*

ALONG THE EXTRA MILE

If anyone forces you to go one mile,
go also the second mile.
Give to everyone who begs from you,
and do not refuse anyone
who wants to borrow from you.

(Matthew 5:41–42, NRSV)

For folk travelling to Iona, there are many stages to the journey. By the time they arrive in Oban they may be moved by the beauty of the views, but also tired and confused. And there's still a ferry, a long bus ride and another ferry to come.

What they need is a nice cup of tea, a decent mug of coffee, maybe food for the journey. A seaside place like Oban isn't short of places to refuel. Some are huge and do roaring business, especially on a rainy day. But I always head for a very small establishment, with an unwieldy name, 'Food from Argyll at the Pier'. It is tucked into the corner of the Calmac terminal building, but run independently by a co-operative made up of food producers throughout the area. The food is local and good. It's cooked and served by young cheerful staff.

There's so little space that they encourage customers to share tables. That means that people have to drop their guard, respond to the questions or stories of other travellers, even put away their mobile phones. Conversations can start from the maps on the walls: one of Argyll, showing where the milk comes from, the cheese is made, the fish is smoked, the coffee is roasted or the beer is brewed; one map of the UK; and another of the world, so that customers can show with a sticker where's home for them. This little café gives the feeling that the people who run it have stories (of food) that they want to share, and they are creating a space where all who come can share their stories.

I think about Jesus, growing up in a village, in a family which each year joined the pilgrimage to Jerusalem, a walk of many miles through the hills. I imagine him as a child listening to tall stories in the marketplace as well as to his people's history in the synagogue. I see Jesus as a grown man not grudging the time people claimed to clamour needs or whisper fears. I smile at him telling stories that everyone would recognise: about how to deal with demanding neighbours, or bullying by a soldier of the Roman occupation (by carrying his pack for an extra mile).

As I'm thinking, I watch one young man, Martin, serving at the counter, his patience with tired and confused customers, his ready smile, his clear interest in the people he's serving. While paying for my coffee, I comment that (even at the end of a busy day) he and his colleagues seem to go out of their way to make these travellers welcome. Martin grins at me. 'It's the least we can do,' he says. 'And I've noticed that it's never crowded along the extra mile.'

Caring God, you know our stories, and the journeys we are making.
Just as you walk with us, help us to accompany others on the road.
Amen

'WHO WILL WALK WITH US?'

If I lift up my eyes towards the hills, where can my help be found?
Your help comes from God, the One who made heaven and earth.
God will keep you from stumbling, your protector is always at hand.
God keeps watch over everyone and never slumbers or sleeps.
God is your guardian at all times, always close at hand.
In daytime no harm shall befall you; at night your life is secure.
God will guard you from evil, and protect your very soul.
God watches our coming and going, now and for evermore.

(Psalm 121, *Iona Abbey Worship Book*)

'Now who will walk with us?' asked the children. Their teachers and parents were lost for words.

Johnny Paton, the parish minister for North Mull, was well known, respected and loved, not just in the church but in the wider community. The Gaelic Choir, the Golf Club, ceilidhs and community meals: he was there, cheerfully joining in, listening to people's confusions or questions, accepting their hospitality and sometimes being the one who made the tea. He was a welcome visitor not only to the Sunday Club at church, but to the day schools. And as each group, about to move up to secondary school, marked this significant moment by climbing Ben More, the highest peak on Mull and a Munro, he walked with them every step of the way.

When Christian Aid, for its 70th anniversary, issued a challenge to supporters to come together to climb 70 of Scotland's highest mountains, Johnny was there with a local group to tackle Ben More. For he greatly valued the work of Christian Aid and was a keen 'Munro-bagger', delighting in the challenge and beauty and the sense of God's presence in the high places.

Just after Easter 2019, on a short holiday, he climbed to the summit of An Teallach, a mountain near Ullapool, alone, and fell and died. As I write this, the community on Mull is still finding ways of dealing with its loss. We know that Christmas will be very different this year for many people, including his courageous wife, Cathy, who chose the psalm above for his funeral service. Like her, we need to witness to a faith which often takes us to hard places, be honest about our mixture of grief and gratitude. Now we too are asking 'Who will walk with us?'

God of the high places
and the down-to-earth here and now,
thank you for watching over our coming and going,
now and always,
thank you for good people who share our journey
and show us your Way.
Amen

'THE CARPENTER'S SON'

Coming to his hometown, he began teaching the people in their synagogue, and they were amazed. 'Where did this man get this wisdom and these miraculous powers?' they asked. 'Isn't this the carpenter's son? Isn't his mother's name Mary, and aren't his brothers James, Joseph, Simon and Judas? Aren't all his sisters with us? Where then did this man get all these things?' And they took offence at him.

(Matthew 13:54–57, NIV)

There is a prayer in the morning Office of the Iona Community which has been used lovingly for many years, but has also caused vigorous controversy, if not offence. Here's the version we now use:

O Christ the Master Carpenter, you at the last, through wood and nails, crafted our whole salvation. Wield well your tools in the workshop of your world so that we who come rough-hewn to your bench may here be fashioned to a truer beauty of your hand. Amen

The prayer, in its different versions, has always felt appropriate to a Community that came into being around the rebuilding of those parts of the Abbey surrounding the cloisters – which George MacLeod called *'the place of the common life'*. Some reading this will remember that, originally, the prayer said that Christ *'purchased our whole salvation'*. This drew on a theology, an idea of a ransom being paid, to which many Community members could not say 'Amen'.

For me – living in a village which was home to some of those craftsmen involved in the rebuilding, including Calum Macpherson, the village carpenter, and remembering the skills and gruff common sense of my own grandfather, away on the Lancashire coast – words like 'crafted' or 'shaped' express profoundly the way God works.

'Shape, lass, shape'

My grandfather was a down-to-earth carpenter;
his words now help me to understand the cross
not as a transaction
but as the work of a craftsman, hands-on,
mending the broken, or taking raw wood,
and seeing what it might become,
cutting with care, planing, shaping
and making the world – once more – whole.

> *God our Maker, our down-to-earth Creator,*
> *bless us as we struggle*
> *to put into words what we believe,*
> *to express our love for you,*
> *who are grandchildren of those who went before,*
> *and your children.*
> *Amen*

SMALL BIRDS FIND A HOME

I long with heartfelt yearning to be within God's house.
My whole being sings for joy to God, the living God.
Even the sparrow finds a home and the swallow makes a nest
where she can rear her brood close to your holy altars …
Happy are those who trust in you as they walk their pilgrim way.

(From Psalm 84, *Iona Abbey Worship Book*)

Here's a story I've been told about the rebuilding of Iona Abbey, one I relish in the retelling. In the south range of the cloisters, nearest to the nave of the Abbey Church, the capitals of the pillars are carved with beautifully observed birds of Iona: swifts, corncrakes, gannets, a falcon. At each corner of the cloisters there's a biblical scene. Here, it is the baptism of Jesus by John. And so there is a bird here, too – the dove of the Holy Spirit, settling on Jesus' hand.

The sculptor, Chris Hall, worked for many months on these meticulous carvings, and he told how, day by day, he was watched by two small birds, a blackbird and a robin, grateful for the crumbs scattered from his daily 'piece' of bread and cheese. The design for the corner capital didn't take up all of the space. There was still a blank surface on the stone. And so he added, in freehand, little portraits of his companions – those who had shared his bread.

Footnotes

Day after day flakes of stone flew in the cloisters
where a sculptor worked on the capitals –
hammer and chisel a breach of the peace;
each time he took his break, quietly enjoying his piece,
robin and blackbird came to share the crumbs.

Commissioned to carve, in the south east corner,
the Baptism of Christ, with dove descending
according to Scripture, the sculptor,
signing off, added two unofficial footnotes –
blackbird and robin, his companions.

Though tools have fallen silent in the cloister,
the birds keep watch from their corner:
skill transforming stone into spirit in the dove,
while these two have their feet on the ground,
as homely as flesh and blood, or daily bread.

> *Creator God, bless the skill that brings stone to life,*
> *and bread that is shared.*
> *Amen*

NEW SHOOTS FROM A FALLEN TREE

Then a branch will grow from the stock of Jesse,
and a shoot will spring from his roots.
On him the spirit of the Lord will rest:
a spirit of wisdom and understanding,
a spirit of counsel and power …
with justice he will judge the poor
and defend the humble in the land with equity.

(Isaiah 11:1–2,4, REB)

In 2005, I was a volunteer with a World Council of Churches programme, spending three months as an Ecumenical Accompanier, based amid the down-to-earth realities of the West Bank village of Jayyous. Early each morning I and my two colleagues from our tiny international team walked with local farmers down to the checkpoint in the Separation Barrier, to see whether the Israeli soldiers would allow them through to work on their family farms – all on the far side of the newly built fence, topped with razor wire. Acres of fertile land and all the wells of Jayyous were cut off by the high fence and the military road that ran alongside. Bulldozers had felled many trees, though some were dug up, to be replanted for decoration in the new settlement which had claimed the land.

I listened to the farmers describing their loss, and, on a rare occasion when we were allowed through the checkpoint, walked among the felled trees.

In no-man's-land

The bulldozers were here a year ago,
destroying an olive grove,
uprooted trees, leaves shed out of season
and crushed limbs scattered on the earth.

As young trees were taken away
for replanting in settlements,
soldiers kept back the farmers:
'When I saw my olive tree
dancing in the jaws of the bulldozer, then I wept.'

The torn earth still lies bare,
a military zone now, a no-man's-land.
What will happen next?
The people wait, steadfast and sad,
and life goes on – strangers are welcomed,
families need to be fed:
branches of the felled trees
fuel backyard ovens, baking daily bread.

Under the moon, behind locked gates
in the farmlands, wild pigs trample and devour
crops that cannot be harvested; a white jackal
runs like death among coils of razor wire.

But under the sun
something is being unlocked
in the desert that was once an olive grove:

from the root, the ravaged stock
of an ancient tree
that seemed gone for ever –

a shoot growing, tender leaves unfolding
like a child's opening hand:
against all despair, a new beginning,
even here, even in no-man's-land.

When I saw it, I wept.

> *O God, when we feel we are walking through no-man's-land,*
> *amid destruction, barrenness and despair,*
> *help us to kneel down and see the signs of life – your life.*
> *Amen*

GOD OUR REFUGE

You, God, have been our refuge from one generation to another.
Before the mountains emerged, before the earth was born,
from everlasting to everlasting, you are God.
You turn back mortals to dust, saying, 'Turn back, earth's children.'
For, in your sight, a thousand years are like a night watch or a single day.

(From Psalm 90, *Iona Abbey Worship Book*)

Some years ago, on a Northumbrian pilgrimage, I was in the company of folk who had misread the tide tables. So we weren't able to cross over to Lindisfarne, where St Cuthbert had lived and inspired many. Instead we went in search of Cuthbert's Cave, one of the places – this one still in sight of the Holy Isle – where members of Cuthbert's community, after his death, took his body. They were seeking a safe place from the Viking raiders, carrying what was most precious to them. They did not know how far they would have to go, what would be his last resting place – or theirs.

Today many aspects of our lives are different (though the tide tables are still relevant!). But the bleakness of winter hills can still be an image of the world in which we live. We still seek places of sanctuary. We still live with uncertainty.

Seeking sanctuary

Somewhere up there to the west,
inland from Lindisfarne, is Cuthbert's Cave:
a safe place for monks manhandling a body on a bier,

saint seeking a resting place
away from the fury of men of iron and fire.

In the hinterland,
low hills of thorn and pine, only a little higher
than the coast which lies open
to welcome and unwelcome guests,
snow lay on the ridge as it does this year.

The brothers must have toiled upwards,
step by step with their burden,
leaving telltale footprints all the way to the cave,
carrying their past – as we do today –
uncertainly into the future; that we share.

A prayer from Durham Cathedral, the shrine of St Cuthbert:

Gracious Lord, we thank you for your servant Cuthbert,
in life a minister of your grace,
in death a channel of your glory.
Grant that in the glad company of your saints
we may journey on in faith, and at the last,
be brought home to your dwelling place in joy;
through our Lord and Saviour Jesus Christ.
Amen

MOMENTS OF WONDER

Praise God from the heavens, praise God in the highest of heavens.
Praise God, all you angels, all you who live in God's presence …
Praise God above the skies in the realms beyond our knowledge …
Praise God, all animals, tame and wild,
creatures that creep and birds that fly.
Praise God, every nation, those who rule and those who judge.
Praise God, men and women alike, young and old together.
Let them praise and honour God's name, whose glory abounds for ever

(From Psalm 148, *Iona Abbey Worship Book*)

On the edge of town, people gathered on a little hill, a slope of sun-baked grass, down which children slid on cardboard, with shrill cries of joy. At the foot of the hill was a school, dominated by the huge ugly chimney of a boiler that would be lit in winter. But now it was balmy late-summer. Families sat together, sharing picnics, talking quietly, listening, scanning the sky, waiting for something … for what?

Suddenly, more shrill cries, from the sky. The swifts were starting to appear, Vaux's swifts, tiny migratory birds: Portland, Oregon is one of the staging points on the long journey they make down the west coast of the Americas. At this point, they need somewhere to roost, and year after year they pause in their migration and circle above Chapman School. The people on the hill gasped with delight as the birds, thousands of them, gathered, swooped overhead, banked and turned. Choreography transformed the evening sky. Then a hawk appeared, patrolling the edge of the flock. The watching people booed. The hawk hurtled into the midst of the birds, but failed to catch one. The watchers cheered. The hawk flew off. The dance went on.

The shrill cries of the tiny birds were lost in the rush of many wings, each time the flock swooped low overhead. Then the huge flock began to rise, up and up, swirling like a column of smoke, until it was now poised over the big chimney. In one movement the birds poured themselves into the mouth of the chimney, to find their roost. As they disappeared, the crowd clapped and cheered and laughed with joy.

Night was falling. As families made their way home, the small birds slept huddled together in the chimney. Ugly, industrial and down-to-earth, this was still a safe place on their long journey. They were in the hands of God.

I'm moved by wonder that such things can happen
in our shared world, in places I'll never see.
I'm moved that my brother, whom I love,
was there, was filled with wonder – and told me.
Amen

LET THE LAND BE GLAD

Let the wilderness and the parched land be glad,
let the desert rejoice and burst into flower.

(Isaiah 35:1, REB)

At midsummer I went to visit a friend, Lucy, who, over the years, has, through hard work, transformed a steep hillside into a garden. She has the tenancy of a croft, and part of the land, more level than the rest, had not been tackled for it was covered in bracken – an invasive fern that's very hard to eradicate. I knew she had been working on it. But when I walked through the gate, I was astonished.

The meadow

As surprising and as fine
as hair on the head of a newborn child,
grasses shimmer and dance on a hillside,
which had been swaddled tight
in bracken's uniform knitted green.
Now there's a lightness on the land:
grasses of many kinds – pale gold, jade,
buff, pink and purple, silver, amber –
seeding, spreading, growing in silence under the sky.

Dominant, invasive bracken left no place
for this beautiful diversity.
But the bracken's gone, gave way to the scythe:

determined human hands cut it again and again
till it gave up the ghost, died back, leaving bare earth
where, under smothering fronds, seeds waited.

Sun touched soil, rain fell, and grasses just grew:
as many as grains of sand, or stars in the sky.
Meadow flowers came, like children out to play
raising bright faces to the sun: buttercups and daisies,
hawkbit and orchids, vetch, clover and yellow rattle,
dancing for a day or summer-long. In time they,
and this multitude of grasses, will die, become hay.

But the seed they set, trusted to the earth,
fed by the rain, will bide its time and rise again.

> *God of the green earth,*
> *bless us with lightness of spirit:*
> *like common grasses and meadow flowers,*
> *may we spring to life and dance in your presence.*
> *Amen*

A ROADSIDE SPRING

As a deer longs for streams of cool water,
so my heart longs for you, O God.
I thirst for you, the living God.
When shall I know that you are near me?

(From Psalm 42, *Iona Abbey Worship Book*)

'Stop if you can, at the bend of the road before the wood. Look for the stone bench. Read the inscription.'

Following the instructions of my friend, who knew the island and its people so much better than I did, I used my eyes as I drove down the road. For a weary walker, it would have been easier to find, and welcome, too: set back against the bank, a stone bench. Nearby was a spring, kept clear of leaves and mud. There, on a back road, on the island of Mull, I read the words carved into the bench:

> 'Margaret Elliot 5 July 1924
> *As the refreshment of water is to the weary traveller,*
> *so were her kindness and courage to the wayfarers of life.'*

I don't know any more about Margaret Elliot, but maybe this is enough.

Maybe you know people like her, quiet embodiments of courage, known and valued for their kindness.

Pause and name them in your hearts. These people have been there for you on your journey. Give thanks for them.

The friend who told me to look for the bench, the spring and the inscription, also persuaded the congregation in Salen, further north on the island, to have simple words of blessing set into the church path. This has been a down-to-earth way of encouraging all who pass by to believe that we can be like Margaret:

Blessing from the church path:

Seek God's love
Know God's love
Accept God's love
Live out God's love
Stay in God's love
Fanaibh ann an Gràdh Dhè

I HAVE CALLED YOU BY NAME

'Do not fear, for I have redeemed you;
I have called you by name – you are mine.
When you pass through the waters I will be with you,
and through the rivers they shall not overwhelm you.'

These words from Isaiah 43:1–2 are written round the rim of the font which stands in the centre of Salisbury Cathedral nave. Designed by William Pye, it is a huge vessel in the shape of a cross, both a work of art, through which water is constantly flowing, and part of the church's tradition in the sacrament of baptism. I return whenever possible, to stand and reflect beside it. It is a very good place to renew baptismal vows.

In a glass darkly

In a glass darkly
the cathedral sees itself reflected;
arches, upside down,
become cupped hands, holding
water still as held breath
yet constantly flowing,
pouring away
and yet replenished;
brimming
and yet contained.

On their different journeys,
young and old,
the fugitive, the called, have fetched up

in the belly of the whale;
under the cathedral's ranged ribs,
whether they like it or not,
they find this heart beating
in the middle of the great building,
this strange sign of beginnings and endings:
and are drawn in
without drowning.

In wonder, one by one,
each approaches, reaches out,
daring to touch the meniscus;
ripples start circles widening
that disturb the whole structure.

Then, as it returns to flowing stillness,
we're stilled as well,
immersed in this mystery
of fountain and font, life and death:
pondering our uniqueness
in its dark glass,
and, with the deep closing over us,
praying our questions.

> *Mysterious God, you are far deeper*
> *than the easy answers at which we clutch.*
> *So in silence, in reflection, in wonder,*
> *we pray our questions.*
> *Amen*

FELL TO EARTH HERE

My security rests in you, O God; let me never be put to shame.
By your saving power deliver me, hear me and keep me safe.
Be a rock of refuge for me to which I can always come …
As long as I can remember, I have put my trust in you.
I have leaned on you since birth, when you brought me out of the womb.
Keep close when energy fails me, as I spend my last years on earth.
Let me wait in constant hope and praise you again and again.

(From Psalm 71, *Iona Abbey Worship Book*)

The Fallen Christ, a sculpture in granite, was inspired by the moment in the traditional Stations of the Cross when Jesus, carrying the cross, falls under its weight. Jim Hughes, a member of the Iona Community, described the desolation of this moment in his poem 'A touching place':

> 'He has travelled all his life to reach here, this very spot.
> His shoulders ache with the weariness of others,
> his brow lacerated by their twisted expectations.'

The renowned Scottish sculptor Ronald Rae carved it out of a single block of granite from Kemnay quarry, Aberdeenshire. The work has been exhibited in various places, including Salisbury Cathedral Close. It was then chosen by Jim and Ronald as a possible gift to Iona – the island community and the intentional Community – in 2008. The gift was accepted and these two men – the worker in stone and the worker in words (in Edinburgh Jim was known as a makar, that is a poet) jointly bore the challenges and cost of transporting it from the mainland and putting it in place outside the MacLeod Centre. It stands on crofting land, where cattle and sheep graze, within view of kitchen door and workshop, by the fence near the compost heap – on common ground, part of our daily lives. Here it is outside the 'vallum' – the ancient earthwork which formed the boundary of the Celtic monastery – outside holiness! Ronald Rae says, '*Christ could not choose where he fell*': this place feels right.

By the time all the documents were signed and arrangements made, Jim was terminally ill and it was midwinter – not a good time for moving a huge piece of granite across the Sound of Iona. But it arrived and he was able to see it lowered into place. His ashes are scattered at this site, as are those of his wife, Margaret (Maggie), who came here for quiet reflection every day she was on Iona until her death in 2015. This has become a down-to-earth holy place.

> *God-with-us,*
> *you are our rock of refuge,*
> *close at hand, down to earth,*
> *as we wait for birth or death,*
> *in daily life, in constant hope.*
> *Amen*

IN GOD'S HANDS

You, O God, are my refuge. Let me never be put to shame.
Bend down your ear and hear me, come quickly to my rescue …
Be a place of safety for me, a rock where I find shelter;
lead and guide me for your own name's sake …
Into your hands I commit my spirit.
Turn your face towards me, with unfailing love defend me,
do not reject me when I call your name. Your goodness knows no limits;
it is kept for all who revere you and turn to you in their need.

(From Psalm 31, *Iona Abbey Worship Book*)

This spring I talked on the phone with two friends, one a sculptor used to hard physical work. But at that time he and his partner were finding it even harder to face her terminal illness. They had walked slowly to a little wood near their home, watching and touching the living things around them. Putting her arms round a sapling, she said she felt comforted by the life that flowed through it. They both compared that to the positive support of medical staff, showing care through human contact – when no words seemed adequate, these folk were not afraid to reach out, to communicate through touch.

But, I wondered, what could I do, being so far away? What can any of us do, confronted by the pain of others? I have only words to offer, the movement of pen across paper, my touch on the keyboard. But maybe – hard as it is to put into words – I can communicate faith that we are all held in God's love. Each of us can pray, with the psalmist, '*Into your hands I commit my spirit.*'

These hands

These hands caress the pregnant rock
feeling where form may yet become:
maker's hands wounded, nearly numb
from years of the granite fighting back.

These hands reach out to embrace a tree:
rough bark, soft moss, buds clutching spring;
mothered by another living thing,
held by an earthy energy.

These hands hold yours, for talk's too much,
when explanations stumble and fall:
head aching, heart breaking, you can feel
outreach of healing human touch.

These hands hold pen, or touch a screen:
to grasp at words, tough discipline,
touched by another's mortal pain,
striving for sense by holding on.

Prayer (based on a blessing from *Iona Abbey Worship Book*):

'Look at your hands – see the touch and the tenderness':
Explore how their lines tell the story of your life.
Hold them open, to receive the richness of the living world,
with which we come in contact every day.
Fold them together, in gratitude for those
whose lives touch ours, whose love holds us.
Cup them, to remember the blessing of God's compassion:
'Into your hands I commit my spirit.'

THE WINGS OF THE MORNING

You search me, God, and you know me;
you know my resting and my rising;
you discern my thoughts from afar ...
Such knowledge is too wonderful for me;
it is beyond my understanding.
Is there anywhere I could go
where you were not there before me? ...
If I took the wings of the morning
and lived beyond the horizon,
even there your hand would find me,
your right hand would hold me fast.

(From Psalm 139, *Iona Abbey Worship Book*)

Yet again I had the privilege and challenge of being an Ecumenical Accompanier in the West Bank Palestinian Territories. This time it was in a village many miles from the Separation Barrier. The challenge for the people of Yanoun was to go on living in the hills where their families had tended orchards of olives and almonds for generations. Now hostile incomers, in settlements illegal even under Israeli law, at that time, wanted them off the land, so that the settlements could expand. Where could the shepherds graze their flocks, when they were confronted by barbed wire and men with guns, court orders and bulldozers? The Israeli settlers claimed that God had given them the land. To the Palestinian shepherds it was home.

In such a potentially violent situation, we were there as peace observers, as a non-violent presence. Sometimes, when the searchlights glared down from watchtowers on the hilltops, it didn't feel a safe place. Yet we respected our neighbours; trusted the Ecumenical Accompaniment Programme, which had placed us there; witnessed the courage of groups like Rabbis for Human Rights, who came to protect the villagers during the olive harvest; knew the encouragement of Palestinian Christians, in cities like Bethlehem. In all these human encounters we were aware of God's presence.

And also, there were moments when what we observed was the sheer beauty of the place. One morning I woke to see a great flock of storks, on the long journey from Africa to Europe, flying high over the land in which Jesus was born, where he lived among human beings with all their conflicts and suffering and injustice, embodying God's love. And where such love can still prevail.

God of journeys,
early in the morning, high over the hills of the West Bank,
a great flock of storks is lit by the rising sun:
with steady wing-beats they fly on, in the mystery of migration.
May we, too, follow your calling to places which challenge us –
where the stones cry out for justice –
until at last we find our home in you.
Amen

A SHELTER TO SAINTS AND SEEKERS

I will bless my Maker at all times,
whose praise is forever on my lips.
My soul will glorify God,
let the humble hear and rejoice …
I looked for God who answered me,
bringing freedom from all my fears.
Those who look to God become radiant,
their faces show no shame.
God hears those who cry for help
and saves them from all their troubles.
The angel of God keeps watch
over those who revere their Maker.
Taste and see: God is good,
a shelter to saints and seekers …

(From Psalm 34, *Iona Abbey Worship Book*)

It was mid-December when the island community gathered in a church-yard not often used now. Funerals here are big events – not for morbid reasons, or simply a desire to 'do the right thing' – but as celebrations of lives fully lived, and of community: an awareness that we all belong together. And also a way of acknowledging, if not answering, the many questions with which we live: Who am I? Why am I here, on this earth? Who cares? And what happens next?

A person who had heard those questions asked often was Bill Pollock, Associate Minister in the north of Mull. He lived on the island for many years, and knew it well. It was he who told me where to look for the

wayside spring, and he who persuaded the people of Salen to set an
encouraging message in their church path (pp.28-29). He was much
loved. For his last years he wasn't able to do the conventional work of a
minister because Parkinson's disease had made his movements awkward
and his words hard to understand. Yet he had a ministry. He accompanied
many on their journey – in his own way. For me he was a friend and a
mentor. He was amused by the Ulva ferryman's description of me as 'the
minister's apprentice' and often used it. So, it was my privilege, after his
death, to listen to the people who were his flock and his friends, then to
speak in the church about his faith, and how it inspired so many of us. He
was buried at a time of year when mortality and the joy of incarnation
mingle.

At Balure
on a bare hillside
in dreich December,
almost the shortest day,
a great tree stands lonely and proud,
guarding the graves of a community barely there.
Broken by gales and time,
the tree's still upstanding,
unique under the open sky.

On the edge of tears, we lay in the earth
a small man with a wayward body –
and a spirit of fire –
who once sheltered under this tree
and said to his friends
'When the time comes, bury me here.'

Here on this island is where
he was fully alive,
full of loyalty and laughter,
grace and truth,
his wayward body
embodying God's glory.

> *'The glory of God is in human beings fully alive.'*
> *Loving God, may this be true of me.*
> *Amen*

BREAD

'The kingdom of heaven is like yeast
that a woman took and mixed into about sixty pounds of flour
until it worked all through the dough.'

(Matthew 13:33, NIV)

In Jesus' time every village, and most homes, had a bake-oven. Jesus watched women like Mary his mother at work daily, adding yeast to flour and setting it to rise.

When I lived in the village of Yanoun, high in the hills above the Jordan Valley, I was invited to spend time with our neighbour, as she went about this daily work. First she took yeast, mixed it with flour and water, and set it to rise. The yeast was bought from the nearby town. The grain, grown in the valley, was ground by a mobile mill. Water came from the village well in an olive grove.

The dough took twelve hours to rise. Then our neighbour went into the bake-house and sat down by the taboon. That's an earth-oven, a depression in the ground, lined with stones that hold the heat, and fired up with dross from the olive-press, which makes very good fuel, the embers of which are piled over the domed cover of the taboon to give out smouldering heat and bake the loaves right through. I sat with her for the time it took, watching her at work and talking gently, as we waited for the flatbread to bake.

Her husband was a farmer, on a small scale, like a Hebridean crofter. He herded sheep and goats, had olive trees and some land under plough – in every case less than before the settlements were built and the outposts appeared on the hilltops around the village. There were six children to feed, and his housebound mother, too.

When the lid was lifted from the taboon, heat rose into the dark little hut, flour dust and smoke danced in a ray of sun. With deft, floured hands, she scooped some of the soft dough from the bowl, flattened it on a floured tray. She lifted it up with both hands; it stretched; without tearing it, she draped it on hot stones, covered it.

I looked at her beautiful tired face, which I could not photograph, out of respect. And, with equal respect, watched the growing pile of bread she was making – and made every day – to feed her family. I was given a crusty, fragrant, still-warm loaf to take home for our household. It was a Sunday morning. For me, this was a sacrament.

> *With-us God, you came to share our human lives*
> *in Bethlehem – 'the house of bread'.*
> *We pray for those who bake bread and break it*
> *on both sides of the wall of separation:*
> *Jewish families gathered for the Shabbat meal,*
> *Christian and Muslim Palestinians,*
> *sharing flatbread fresh from the taboon.*
> *You are Living Bread, broken that all might be fully alive,*
> *so we pray for the day when all your children*
> *will be free to share their daily bread together, in peace.*
> *Amen*

FEET IN FLOWING WATER

You, God, are my shepherd;
I need nothing more.
You let me lie down in green pastures,
you lead me beside still waters;
there you revive my spirit.
You guide me in the right paths,
for you are true to your name.

(From Psalm 23, *Iona Abbey Worship Book*)

Soon after my friend was widowed, we were talking together about the places where she and her husband had loved to be; places where they felt their spirits being revived. As she had accompanied him in the last months, she said, she was grateful that there had been time to do and say what was needed. But of course it was not an easy journey, and life became focused on small things, located close to home.

For some time there had been little opportunity to go out into the hills where they used to enjoy walking together, beside lively tumbling burns (anything but still waters!). Now, a month after the funeral, she was looking forward to taking a few days in the Highlands.

'It's so long,' she said, 'since I put my feet in a burn.'

Blessing

May you hear once more the song of the burn
beckoning – and be free to respond.
May you walk where it weaves remembered joy
with the changed pattern of your present life.
May you see posies of foam like rowan blossom,
forming, flowing on peat-brown currents.
May you take off your shoes and feel cool water
caress and bless your tired feet.
Amen

BELONGING AND BALANCE

Help us to plan our years,
so that wisdom may grow in our hearts.
How long, O God, till you return to us?
Have pity on your people.
Show us your love when morning breaks
and we will be joyful all our days.
For all the days when we have known misfortune,
balance them with days of joy.
Let your care be evident to your servants
and your glory to the next generation.
Let your favour rest upon us
and bless the work of our hands.

(Psalm 90, from *Iona Abbey Worship Book*)

There was a play advertised in the village hall. It was called *Here I Belong*, and was happening in this homely familiar place. On the posters there was this message: 'There's a celebration in the local hall and you're invited – there will be cake.'

The play had begun its tour in Mull Theatre, then moved to a real village hall, in Bunessan where I live. That night the elements raged, with gales, thunder, lightning and rain – weather more suited to a well-known Scottish Play than to a gentle, funny, poignant story of a community like our own. More than 40 people turned up, and sat round tables set up as though for a ceilidh, while the cast of two moved around us, spreading cloths, putting up bunting, arranging flowers and teacups. The action covered seventy years of one woman's life, in which the milestones were marked by gatherings in a village hall: a celebration after the war, weddings, the Coronation, a memorial, a 90th birthday.

One actor played Elsie, the central figure, the other was in turn a close friend, then a young woman who had left the village for London, then a new, posh neighbour, and finally Elsie's carer. While these characters came and went, Elsie never left the stage, but between scenes she changed just one item of clothing, which took us into the next stage of her life. Her ageing was much more than a costume change. Her body-language, so lively at the beginning, became stiffer, more hesitant. Without using makeup, her face changed. But this was not a caricature of age, for (just as in real life) it was possible all the time to see the same Elsie, a vulnerable and yet resilient human being, who never lost her sense of humour.

Everyone to whom I spoke, old and young, was enthusiastic about the play. Some were in tears, too. Creatively, it has led to some deep conversation, about belonging in a community, about balance in our lives. Right at the end, each night, there was the cake we'd been promised. Our village tasted a treat in *Here I Belong*, but there was something more sustaining, too – a reflection on what it means to be human.

God of our changing lives,
may we go on learning where we belong,
who cares for us and that we, your children,
are sustained by your constant love.
Amen

SINGING FOR JUSTICE

Sing to God a new song,
for God has done marvellous things,
revealing true salvation
in the sight of all nations …
Praise the God who comes
to judge the earth with justice
and govern its people with fairness.

(From Psalm 98, *Iona Abbey Worship Book*)

It was a sunny September Friday in Iona. As the pilgrims and tourists came off the ferry, there at the head of the jetty they were greeted by a demonstration – up to 80 people on the grassy slope below Iona Cottage. There were banners and placards and songs. The schoolchildren were there, having brought a wheelbarrow of plastic rubbish picked up on the beaches. Now they were waving their messages about caring for the planet. There were island families with babes in arms; grandparents, elders of the local community; Iona Community staff and volunteers; a group of tuneful young Germans from Iona Hostel; guests from the hotels; locals from neighbouring Mull and Iona folk who had closed their local businesses in order to join in this 'Climate Strike'. It was 20 September, 2019. All over the world people were taking to the streets, with messages of challenge to the people in power, with banners and songs, in the capital cities of Europe, filling the centre of London, marching in Edinburgh, across Scotland – and in Iona too. The call had come from the young, from Greta Thunberg and her generation.

So we sang on the jetty in Iona. All ages together, islanders and visitors, we sang for the children's future; we sang for the planet; we sang to send a message to the world's leaders; we sang for climate justice. That song is our prayer. *Amen*

THE TURNING YEAR

Sing a new song, all the earth;
sing a new song to God.

(from Psalm 96, *Iona Abbey Worship Book*)

A year and a half ago the island of Ulva was in the news. With support from the Scottish Land Fund, a 'community buyout' had put it into the hands of local people. It is a beautiful wild place, an island only a short distance from the coast of Mull, with many miles of shore, heather-covered hills, deciduous woodland, and neglected pastures overrun with bracken. The few people who live there have been welcoming walkers and bird-watchers who come over for the day on the small ferry. There's a café offering local produce and a thatched cottage with displays about the island's history. But now there are plans to bring more young families to live on the island, to increase housing and job opportunities: to bring the place back to life.

People value their old church, no longer in regular use. But services there are seen as opportunities to celebrate community. Folk come from all over Mull, tourists too: many of whom seldom go to church. Together they walk up the track through the woods. At Easter this year, the theme of our worship (reflecting the season, Ulva's potential, and resurrection hope) was 'Spring to Life'.

This was our opening prayer:

> *Living, loving God, we gather here on this green island.*
> *After the long cold sleep of winter,*

at last young leaves are unfurling on the trees,
primroses and celandines are in bloom along the track.
We praise you for their beauty, and the promise they bring of new life.

We gather here in an old building,
that has sheltered worshippers over the years,
has provided space for baptisms and funerals and weddings,
where Sunday by Sunday psalms were sung, the Bible was read,
where sins were confessed, thanksgiving expressed,
the wider world remembered.
Out of that wider world we gather here.
And we know that sometimes
this building has stood empty for many months,
and sometimes passers-by have wondered what was its point,
or visitors have relished its peace and guessed at its memories.
And we can see that for a time this was used as a Community Centre,
a space for dancing and feasting and mutual care;
we know that lively worship in more recent years –
harvest festivals, Easter celebrations, Christmas –
had room for dogs and lambs as well as people,
and for stories like the piano that fell through the floor –
and laughter.
Because laughter is part of the healing life of your Spirit.

And here, here, we offer our praise to you:
God, who contains the universe
and created the earth, our home;
Jesus Christ, born into a down-to-earth community,

whose life embodied your love –
God-with-us, who died and then sprang to life again,
bringing hope to all humanity;
we offer praise in the power of your Holy Spirit,
inspiring, comforting, encouraging,
and present with us now.
Amen

BROKEN GLASS ANGELS

And there were shepherds living out in the fields nearby,
keeping watch over their flocks at night.
An angel of the Lord appeared to them,
and the glory of the Lord shone around them,
and they were terrified.
But the angel said to them, 'Do not be afraid.
I bring you good news that will cause great joy for all the people.
Today in the town of David a Saviour has been born to you;
he is the Messiah, the Lord.
This will be a sign to you:
You will find a baby wrapped in cloths and lying in a manger.'

(Luke 2:8–12, NIV)

Give your life over to God, who will bring out the best in you.
Your integrity will be clear and as bright as the noonday sun.

(From Psalm 37, *Iona Abbey Worship Book*)

On the shores of Iona and Mull, people pick up sea-glass, smoothed by the waves. We wonder at its beauty and use it for meditation or decoration.

Each Advent I hang glass decorations in my window, a star, an angel, a dove, but these have come from far away, from Bethlehem. A handout from the craft-workshop at the International Centre of Bethlehem explains how they are made:

'These art pieces are made out of glass, fragments of broken bottles thrown away or glass destroyed during the Israeli invasion of Bethlehem. Human hands pick them up from the rubble, then they are put together (in ICB workshops) by some of the poorest of the poor in Bethlehem. These art pieces tell all about "the hopes and fears of all the years" that people have in Bethlehem today. The broken glass pieces are a sign of the brokenness of our world. Through the Incarnation God brought the divine and the human back together, taking what seems to be worthless and hopeless and transforming it into a beautiful and whole creation. It is this incarnation, which took place here in Bethlehem two thousand years ago, which gives us the strength to continue to look for broken lives and hopes and to transform them into works of art like angels, messengers of justice, peace and dignity.'

Debris of our lives,
breaking waves and abrasive sand –
slow sea change,
transforming over time
these jagged edges.

Now, smooth in your hand or mine,
each fragment is jewel-bright:
an angel flies, a dove hovers, a star refracts the light –
what's broken finds wholeness,
shards become a sign.

Creative Spirit, come,
and as you transform our broken world,
may our lives catch the light.
Amen

WORSHIP IN EAST JERUSALEM

I was glad when they said to me
'Let us go to the house of God.'
Now we are inside the gates
of Jerusalem, God's strong city …
Pray for the peace of Jerusalem.
Peace to all those who love you.
Peace be within your walls,
and safety in your streets.
To all of those I love,
my greeting is 'Peace be with you.'

(From Psalm 122, *Iona Abbey Worship Book*)

'As-Salaam-Alaikum' was the greeting of the deacon at the door of the Catholic Orthodox Church near the Damascus Gate, 'Peace be with you.' The worshippers, including myself – newly arrived in East Jerusalem with no Arabic except these words – wished him peace in return: 'Wa-Alaikum-Salaam.'

What did I know about Jerusalem? As little as the Celtic monks who heard pilgrims' tales of the Holy Places, and who then wove the floor plan of the Church of the Holy Sepulchre into one of the ornate 'carpet pages' of the Book of Kells. They would never see that shrine, but they imagined it.

Gazing at that statement of faith which is also a work of art, I'd been intrigued by the angels whose worship was expressed by the long-handled circular fans they held aloft. I'd never seen such things. I learned they were called 'Flabella' – something belonging to a long-lost way of life. Yet here, in the little church near the Damascus Gate, warm with crowded humanity, fragrant with incense, bright with the morning sun, I saw one in use, in an act of worship in which I had been welcomed to share.

Flabella

Shaken, not by an angel in the Book of Kells, long ago,
but by a grey-haired acolyte
in a congregation in Jerusalem, here and now:
a chime like ice falling
from the twigs of birch trees as the sun rises;
incense rising like mist, as the priest breaks the Host.
January sun streams through high windows
and 'Light of light' sing the people
in their Sunday best, in Arabic; and, after,
the acolyte by the candled altar
shakes the flabellum once more, above bright Sunday faces,
so the little bells resound like angels' laughter.

Peace, is our prayer:
peace to friend and stranger,
peace to our world.
Amen

MESSAGES OF LOVE

All at once there was with the angel a great company of the heavenly host,
singing praise to God: 'Glory to God in the highest heaven
and on earth peace to all in whom he delights.'

(Luke 2:13,14, REB)

Many people still send, and relish receiving, Christmas mail. Sending cards is a tradition less than 200 years old. Maybe 50 years ago it started to be overtaken by circular letters – but still in envelopes with stamps. Today folk find it much more efficient to communicate by e-mail, or e-cards – or many delightful and dreadful variations of these.

More important than the form they take, is the purpose and content of these messages. Are they merely (and wearily) observing a convention, or are their words personal and their pictures chosen with care? Are they flippant or boastful or corporate? Are they ways of supporting a good cause, or lovingly handmade? Secular or religious? Is their message at heart one of peace? Christmas communication varies as much as we human beings do: what we believe and how we live.

These cards are also, in my imagination, like flocks of birds, migrants, filling the air at a particular time of year, coming from far away, into our lives.

Christmas post

First, it was swallows, gathering on wires
as bracken rusted and air had an edge.
For the winter, puffins had put out to sea;

and no more calling from corncrakes,
posted early to Africa.
Suddenly the sky's full of wings again:
murmurations of migrant starlings,
wild geese clamouring as they fly in,
a flock of whooper swans, a single egret –
rare visitors arriving from distant places.

They bring news of different lives,
changing seasons, a changing world;
the flock flickering like ticker-tape,
they cross frontiers, unstoppable,
they keep coming, keep coming.

Like envelopes addressed to us,
in each bird-body a small beating heart;
folded paper embodying the wonder
of expectancy coming down to earth.
Just as the days darken,
there's this lightening of spirit
as messages of love keep coming:
the sky full of wings.

> *Spirit of community and communication,*
> *may we recognise and relish your presence:*
> *whether it's in flights of angels or flocks of birds,*
> *radio broadcasts or Christmas post –*
> *or simply family and friends,*
> *with all their messages of love.*
> *Amen*

LIGHT OUT OF DARKNESS

In the beginning was the Word,
and the Word was with God
and the Word was God …
In him was life,
and that life was the light of all humankind.
The light shines in the darkness,
and the darkness has not overcome it.

(John 1:1–2, 4–5, NIV)

As our Advent journey brings us close to Christmas, it would be appropriate to turn to one of the readings from the Lectionary for Christmas Day: John 1:1–14.

Read this passage reflectively.

Close your eyes after each sentence.

Then open them on the light of the place where you are, here and now.

Read it as a message of hope breaking into your here and now.

Then you may also want to use this prayer. It was written from the place where I live now and try to follow God's Way, a shabby village by a busy road, on a remote island. Like Palestine 2000 years ago it is a place 'on the edge'. And that's where God comes to us, in human form, as living Word, as light out of darkness.

A dawn prayer from the Hebrides

Alpha and Omega, you were there at our beginning
and you will be there at our end.
Coasts and islands wait for the dawn,
the dark sea surrounds us like waters in the womb,
like the last river we have to cross.
We wait, trusting, seeing the sky lightening, horizons opening up,
colours of dawn dancing across restless waves.
Spirit of God, in Jesus, you shared our birth and our mortality,
and you are present with us now. We wait.
The clouds become bright, the rocks glow,
our hearts catch fire with sudden joy – the sun rises.
Rise in our hearts, we pray, today and every day.
Amen

SOURCES

Iona Abbey Worship Book, Wild Goose Publications, 2017 © Iona Community.

Passages from NRSV copyright 1989, Division of Christian Education of the National Council of the Churches of Christ in the United States of America. Used by permission. All rights reserved.

Scripture quotations taken from The Holy Bible, New International Version® NIV® Copyright © 1973 1978 1984 2011 by Biblica, Inc. TM Used by permission. All rights reserved worldwide.

Scripture quotations taken from the Revised English Bible, copyright © Cambridge University Press and Oxford University Press 1989. All rights reserved.

Some poems in this book have appeared in *Between High and Low Water*, Jan Sutch Pickard, Wild Goose Publications; *A Pocket Full of Crumbs*, Jan Sutch Pickard, Wild Goose Publications; and *May Contain Eagles*, Jan Sutch Pickard, Oystercatcher/Gillebrighde.

The text on page 53 comes from the Al-Kahf Arts and Crafts Centre in the International Centre of Bethlehem.

Jan Sutch Pickard is a storyteller, poet and preacher, living on the Isle of Mull and involved in many ways in community life there. She is called to the laity – the ministry of the whole people of God. Many years ago she worked for the Methodist Church as an editor, and then for the Iona Community in the MacLeod Centre and Abbey, latterly as Warden of the Abbey. Iona is a 'sending place' and soon after leaving there she volunteered with the World Council Of Churches' Ecumenical Accompaniment Programme, serving on different occasions in two West Bank villages. Since then she has been involved in advocacy for those working for peace in Israel/Palestine, in studying the situation and in prayer. Enjoying every aspect of family life, she currently lives too far from her grandchildren, to whom this is dedicated. She is blessed, though, by an extended family of friends, including some whose stories are told here.

Wild Goose Publications, the publishing house of the Iona Community established in the Celtic Christian tradition of Saint Columba, produces books, e-books, CDs and digital downloads on:

- holistic spirituality
- social justice
- political and peace issues
- healing
- innovative approaches to worship
- song in worship, including the work of the Wild Goose Resource Group
- material for meditation and reflection

For more information:

Wild Goose Publications
The Iona Community
21 Carlton Court, Glasgow, G5 9JP, UK

Tel. +44 (0)141 429 7281
e-mail: admin@ionabooks.com

or visit our website at
www.ionabooks.com
for details of all our products and online sales